Marvelous Memories

Paper Keepsake Creations

by Kara L. Laughlin

CAPSTONE PRESS
a capstone imprint

Table *of* Contents

Fold it.
Tear it.
Make it.
Keep it.

Our lives are full of paper. Think about the ticket stubs, postcards, posters, and programs you've collected. These papers might not have meaning to everyone, but they might be really valuable to you. What can you do with these slips of paper? Transform them into beautiful projects you can keep and display.

Ready to get started? Start by gathering those special papers. Grab sheets of music, maps, posters, and anything else you can think of. You can also use colorful paper or printed card stock found at craft and office supply stores. Next get those craft tools ready. You probably already have basic paper craft tools like scissors, rulers, and craft glue. Any supplies you don't have can be found at most hardware, craft, or office supply stores.

As you work on these projects, add your own personal touch. After all, these projects should be uniquely your own, just like the memories they're keeping.

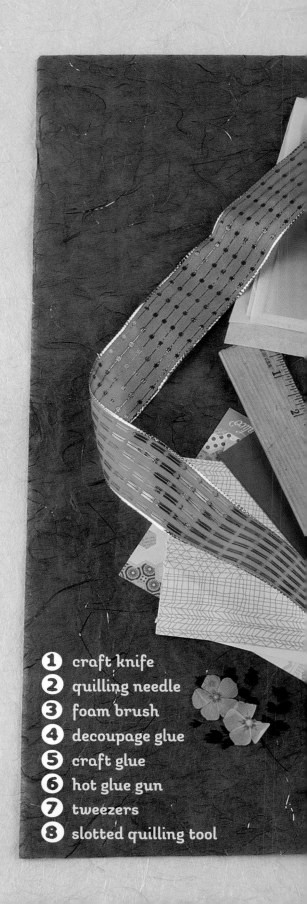

1. craft knife
2. quilling needle
3. foam brush
4. decoupage glue
5. craft glue
6. hot glue gun
7. tweezers
8. slotted quilling tool

Light It Up

Keep the memory of a treasured trip shining in your mind and in your room. This lamp will make any dreary day fabulous.

1. Wrap the map around the lamp shade, adjusting it so your trip route is on the shade.

2. Use a pencil to mark the map all the way around the top and bottom edges of the shade. Mark an X on the top and bottom edges where the map overlaps.

3. Draw a straight line connecting the two Xs. Then cut along your pencil marks to cut the map to fit the shade.

4. Paint a thin layer of decoupage glue on the shade.

5. Carefully wrap the cut map around the shade. Smooth out wrinkles and allow it to dry.

6. Poke earrings through the shade at places on the map where you stopped. Put the backs on the earrings to hold them in place.

7. Wrap embroidery floss around the earring posts to mark your route.

8. Cut images from travel brochures, restaurant menus, postcards, and other paper souvenirs from your trip. Brush decoupage glue on the back of each image, and press them onto the map.

9. Brush a layer of decoupage glue over the entire lamp shade. Let dry.

10. Use hot glue to attach ribbon or cord to the shade as an added decoration.

Materials:

road map

flat-sided lamp shade

foam brush

decoupage glue

post earrings with backs

embroidery floss

paper souvenirs from a trip

hot glue

ribbon or upholstery cord

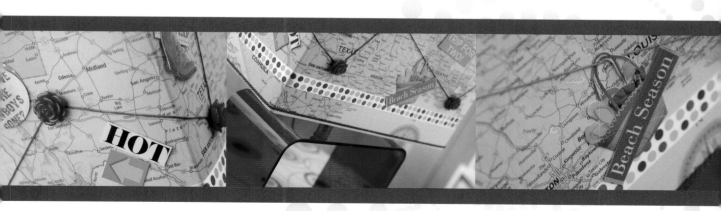

Hanging Notes

Whether you like country, pop, rock, or oldies, this music-inspired wall art will rock your world.

One hand in the air
for the big city.

CITY

DREAMS

Street lights, big dreams
all looking pretty

No place in the world
can compare

WORLD

1. Place a card stock square pattern side down on your work space. With a craft knife and ruler, score a line ½ inch (1 centimeter) from each side of the square. The score lines will make small squares at each corner. Cut out these squares. Then fold the card stock back along the score lines.

2. Tape inside the corners of the card stock to make an open square box.

3. Repeat steps 1–2 with the other two squares of card stock.

4. Turn the boxes patterned sides up. Glue the squares of sentimental paper to the boxes at fun angles.

5. Cut out three musical notes or other fun shapes from the watercolor paper. Use rubber stamps to color the edges of the cutout shapes. Let them dry.

6. Write song lyrics on plain paper. Cut them out with decorative-edge scissors.

7. Glue the song lyric strips to the card stock boxes. Then use alphabet stickers or stencils to call out a word from the lyrics on each square.

8. Cut 12 strips from scrap paper that are ¼x2 inches (.6x5 cm). Glue the ends of two strips together to form two sides of a square. Fold the strips back and forth over each other to form a springy column. Repeat with the other strips.

9. Glue four columns to the back of one paper shape. Glue the other ends of the columns to a card stock box. The paper shape will float a bit above the box. Repeat with the other shapes.

10. Cut a 31-inch (79-cm) piece of ribbon. Hot glue the boxes to the ribbon, leaving 1 inch (2.5 cm) between each box and 4 inches (10 cm) at the top and bottom. Fold the top and bottom ribbon ends over into loops and hot glue in place.

Materials:

3 7-inch (18-cm) squares of patterned card stock

craft knife

invisible tape

craft glue

3 5-inch (13-cm) squares cut from sentimental paper such as concert programs or flyers

heavy watercolor paper

rubber stamps and ink pad

permanent marker

plain paper

decorative-edge scissors

alphabet stickers or stencils

4-inch (10-cm) wide ribbon

hot glue

Captivating Container

With a few petals from a dance corsage or a nature walk, this bowl will hold your makeup—and your memories.

1. Rip the construction paper into tiny pieces and put them in a large bowl. Pour in just enough water to cover the paper. Mix it with your hand to be sure that all the paper gets wet. Let the mixture sit at least eight hours.

2. Pour the paper and water mixture into a blender and blend until smooth pulp forms. Pour the mixture into a bowl.

3. Grab a handful of pulp. Squeeze water out of the pulp over an empty bowl. Squeeze until the pulp is as wet as a damp sponge. Place the pulp in a clean bowl. Repeat with the rest of the pulp.

4. Add the salt, glitter, craft glue, and flowers to the bowl of pulp. Use your hands to gently mix everything together.

5. Cover the inside of a small bowl with petroleum jelly. Smooth a layer of plastic wrap over the jelly, with enough extra to fold over the edges of the bowl. Smooth another layer of petroleum jelly over the plastic.

6. Line strips of tissue paper inside the bowl to make stripes. Use as many or as few as you'd like. Trim the strips so they don't overlap the edge.

7. Press the paper pulp into the bowl over the tissue paper. Keep pressing the pulp into the bowl until the whole bowl is covered. Smooth the edge of the paper pulp by gently pinching it.

8. To make a colored lip on your bowl, press tissue paper strips along the paper pulp's edge. Gently fold the paper around the edge of the paper pulp. Use a fingernail or knife to tuck it between the pulp and the plastic wrap.

9. Let your bowl dry for three to four days. When it is completely dry, pull on the plastic wrap to release your bowl from the mold. Peel the plastic wrap off your bowl.

10. Brush decoupage glue over the entire bowl. Let it dry completely. Repeat two more times.

Materials:

four pieces of construction paper

water

1 teaspoon (5 mL) salt

2 teaspoons (10 mL) glitter

¼ cup (60 mL) craft glue

¼ cup (60 mL) flower petals or small flowers

3- to 4-inch (8- to 10-cm) wide bowl to use as a mold

petroleum jelly

plastic wrap

brightly colored tissue paper, cut into ¼-inch (.6-cm) strips

foam brush

decoupage glue

Tip: For a smoother bowl, use toilet paper instead of construction paper.

Timeline Journal

Time flies when you're having fun. Remember all the details of a special event with this unique journal.

1. Lay one piece of cardboard on the wrapping paper. Wrap the cardboard like a gift, then unfold. Brush decoupage glue on both sides of the cardboard. Lay the cardboard back on the wrapping paper and refold. Secure the ends of the paper with glue if needed. Repeat with the other cardboard piece.

2. Lay the drawing paper out on your workspace. Fold the left-hand side over 5 inches (13 cm) and crease. Then fold that section under 5 inches (13-cm) and crease. Continue to accordion fold the paper until you reach the end.

3. Unfold the drawing paper stack and lay it out on your workspace. Draw a straight line 4 inches (10 cm) from the bottom across the length of the paper, stopping at the crease just before the last section.

4. On the left-hand side, write the first date of a special trip or other event along the line you drew. Glue photos, newspaper clippings, or other paper souvenirs around the date. Write any notes or comments you have on the page too. Continue adding dates and memories to the pages in the order they occurred. Leave the last 5-inch (13-cm) section of paper blank. When done, refold the paper. When folded, the top of the stack should be blank.

Materials:

2 9x5½-inch (23x14-cm) pieces of cardboard

wrapping paper

foam brush

decoupage glue

8½x50-inch (22x127-cm) piece of drawing paper, cut from a roll

permanent markers

glue stick

photos and other paper souvenirs from a special event

2 9x5½-inch (23x14-cm) pieces of tissue paper in two different colors

alphabet stickers

3½x 5½-inch (9x14-cm) piece of vellum

hot glue

additional embellishments, such as extra vellum, stick-on decorations, flowers, or ribbon

5. Apply glue to the blank front page of the folded paper stack. Lay one decorated cardboard piece on top of the glue and press gently.

6. Turn the stack over and apply glue to the bottom page. Attach the second cardboard piece to this glued page. Turn the project back over.

7. Brush decoupage on the front cover. Lay a piece of tissue paper on the glue. Brush more glue over the paper and cover it with a second piece of tissue. Let dry.

8. Use alphabet stickers to put a title for your journal on the piece of vellum. Hot glue the vellum to the cardboard cover. If wanted, decorate the front cover with other vellum cutouts, tissue paper, stick-on elements, flowers, or ribbons.

Locket of Love

Keep those you love close to your heart. Craft this lovely locket from paper, and fill it with a picture you can treasure every day.

1. Use a heart-shaped paper punch to cut two hearts from card stock and one from a photo. (Or trace a heart-shaped cookie cutter and cut them out by hand.)

2. Stick two paper reinforcement rings together. Glue the ring to the top left of one of the paper hearts. Half of the reinforcement should hang over the edge. Repeat for the top right and middle of the heart.

3. Glue the photo over the paper heart and reinforcements.

4. Cut the other paper heart in half from top to bottom.

5. Turn the heart with the photo upside down. Brush the back of this heart with decoupage glue. Apply glue to both sides of the heart halves too.

6. Cut a 6-inch (15-cm) piece of ribbon. Glue the ribbon to the back of one heart half near the straight edge. Put the ribbon at the same height as the reinforcement rings on the photo heart. Repeat for the other heart half.

7. Cut two ¼x1-inch (.6x2.5-cm) strips and two ¼x ½-inch (.6x1-cm) strips from scrap paper. Fold one strip in half. Then fold each end back to the fold. When you lay the paper on its side, it should look like a W. Repeat with the other strips.

Materials:

2-inch (5-cm) wide heart-shaped paper punch or small heart cookie cutter

card stock

photo

¼-inch (.6-cm) paper reinforcement rings

craft glue

foam brush

decoupage glue

thin ribbon

scrap paper

clear, dimensional paper sealant

paper hole punch

decorative paper

Tip: Always let the glue dry before moving on to the next step.

8. Cover the photo with dimensional paper sealant. While it is still wet, place the short paper strips on the bottom left and right of the photo. Place the longer paper strips on the top left and right of the photo. Attach each strip only up to the first fold. Pop any air bubbles in the sealant with a toothpick.

9. Glue the ends of the strips to the split hearts so that the heart pieces close over the photo.

10. Thread the ribbon from the left heart piece through the left reinforcement ring. Repeat on the right. Tie the ribbons together at the back of the locket. When you pull on the ribbon, the heart halves will slide open to reveal the photo underneath.

11. Punch out small circles from the decorative paper. Glue them to the heart halves as decoration.

12. Thread a 20-inch (51-cm) piece of ribbon through the ring at the top of the heart. Knot the ends together.

Photo Ornament

Friends are forever with this keepsake ornament. It will be a treasured reminder of your bond for years to come.

1. Using your 1½-inch (4-cm) paper punch, cut out seven circles from each of the different scrapbook papers. (You can also cut your circles by hand, using a small can for tracing.)

2. Take one of the circles and write a "T" for template on it. This circle won't be used in the actual ornament. Fold the edges of your template toward the center to make a triangle. The corners of the triangle should be on the edge of the circle. All three sides should be the same length. (This might take a few tries.)

3. Place each of the circles on the template. Fold the circles, using the template as a guide.

4. Glue 10 triangles to each other in a straight line by their folded tabs. The points and bases of the triangles will alternate. Make the line into a ring by gluing the last triangle to the first at the side tabs.

5. To make the top of the ornament, glue five triangles together side by side, with all of the points facing up. Do the same with the last five triangles to make the bottom. You should have two domes.

6. Glue the five remaining tabs on the top dome to the five tabs on the top of the ring.

7. Thread a ribbon through a needle. Start the needle inside the ball and poke it up through a corner in the dome. Then pass the ribbon back down into the dome to make a loop on the top of the ornament. Tie the ribbon ends in a knot, and glue the knot to the inside of the ball.

8. Glue the remaining dome to the bottom of the ring, as in step 6.

9. Use a ½-inch (1-cm) circle punch to cut circles from the photos. (You can also cut these circles by hand, using a nickel for tracing.) Glue these photo circles in as many of the ornament segments as you like. Let dry.

Materials:

1½-inch (4-cm) circle paper punch or a small can for tracing

decorative scrapbook paper in three different colors or designs

glue stick

10-inch (25-cm) string or ribbon

needle

½-inch (1-cm) circle paper punch or a nickel for tracing

photos of friends

Party Scrapbook

Some parties you never want to forget. After your bash, reuse the gift wrap and ribbons to make this scrapbook. It will be like holding your party in your hands.

1. Cut 10 4½x6-inch (11x15-cm) pieces from card stock. Cut two pieces of the same size from cardboard.

2. Use a piece of wrapping paper to cover the top half of one cardboard piece. Fold the paper over the edges to cover both sides, and trim the paper as needed. Unfold. Do the same with a different piece of wrapping paper on the bottom half of the piece and unfold.

3. Brush decoupage glue over both sides of the cardboard piece. Rewrap the wrapping papers around the piece. Cover the seam with a length of ribbon, secured with craft glue.

4. Repeat steps 2–3 with the other cardboard piece.

5. Punch five holes through the cardboard pieces, ½ inch (1 cm) from the left edge. Do the same with the card stock pages.

6. Decorate one cardboard piece with more ribbons, punched pieces from greeting cards, and other elements that fit your party's theme. This will be the book's front cover.

7. Fill the inside pages with photos, stickers, and other souvenirs from the party. Write details about the party on the pages too, so you'll never forget the fun you had!

8. Stack the front cover, pages, and back cover together so the holes align.

9. Thread a 28-inch (71-cm) piece of ribbon through the bottom holes of the book. Make the ribbon ends even, then tie a knot at the spine of the book.

10. Lace the ribbon up the book's spine, ending with a double-knotted bow. Glue beads or charms to the ends of the ribbon if desired.

Materials:

solid color card stock

cardboard

wrapping paper from a party

foam brush

decoupage glue

ribbon from a party

craft glue

paper hole punch

greeting cards from a party

stick-on paper embellishments to suit your theme

photos and other paper souvenirs from a party

beads or charms (optional)

Tip: When binding your book, use binder clips to keep the pages lined up.

Keepsake Box

Special treasures deserve a special home. Create a keepsake box that's as pretty as the things you put inside.

1. Turn the box lid upside down on a piece of copy paper. Trace around the lid. Set this paper aside.

2. Turn the lid right-side up. Lay a strip of tissue paper on the lid. Brush decoupage glue over the strip, smoothing the wrinkles. Continue adding paper until the lid and its sides are covered. Trim pieces that go past the edges. Allow the lid to dry.

3. Cut decorative paper to fit around the outside of the box. Brush decoupage glue on the box and attach the paper.

4. Inside the lid tracing, draw a design for the top of your box. Keep at least ⅛ inch (.3 cm) of space between all the lines.

5. Place your drawing on a cutting mat. Use a craft knife to cut out the picture you drew. If you accidentally cut off a section, tape the pieces back together and keep going. This will be your stencil.

6. Attach the stencil to patterned paper with repositionable tape.

7. Place the stencil and paper on the cutting mat. Use your stencil to guide you as you cut out your design from the patterned paper. Don't worry if you accidentally cut too far or tear the paper. You can repair it later.

8. Gently remove the stencil and tape from the cut out design.

9. Brush a thin layer of decoupage glue on the lid. Carefully press your cut paper on the lid. If any parts of the design were torn or cut off, use the brush and glue to fix the damage. Gently smooth out any wrinkles.

10. Brush three layers of decoupage glue over the paper cutting, allowing the glue to dry between coats.

Materials:

small cardboard or paper mache box with lid

copy paper

tissue paper cut into strips

foam brush

decoupage glue

decorative paper

self-healing cutting mat or piece of corrugated cardboard

craft knife

repositionable tape

Tips: If you need to cut out a clean point, cut toward the point from both sides. Don't try to turn the corner.

Don't try to cut all the way through the paper the first time. Instead, work on getting the line right. Then go over it again.

Four-Square Photo Frame

Photos are like friends. They're a lot of fun when you get them all together. This stacked frame has room for everyone.

Create the frame:

1. Fold one square paper in half horizontally, patterned side facing out. Unfold. Then fold in half vertically and unfold.

2. Fold each corner into the center of the X made by the creases. Unfold. Fold each corner to the crease made by the previous fold. Unfold. You should now have two creases in each corner.

3. Fold each corner point to the closest crease. Without unfolding, fold the corner again to the second crease.

4. Turn the paper so one corner points up. Slip a photo into the center of the frame.

5. Fold each corner backward 1 inch (2.5 cm). Punch a hole into the center of each corner.

6. Repeat steps 1–5 to make a total of four frames.

7. Push a wooden dowel through the left and right corner holes of two paper frames. The frames should be strung on the dowel with their middle sides touching. Repeat with another dowel and the other two frames.

8. Use another pair of dowels to connect the top and bottom frames in the same way. Make sure the dowels extend ½ inch (1 cm) below the bottom of the frames.

9. At each hole, secure the dowels with glue.

10. To make the stand, fold the strip of scrapbook paper in half to make a 2x6-inch (5x15-cm) strip. Fold the ends of the paper back to make two 1-inch (2.5-cm) tabs.

11. Lay the strip down so the folded edge is on the left and the tabs are on the right. Measure ½ inch (1 cm) from the bottom corner of the folded edge. Make a mark. Use a straight edge to draw a diagonal line from that mark to the bottom right hand corner. Cut on that line, going through the tabs. Glue the flaps to the back of the bottom frames, behind the vertical dowels.

Materials:

4 8-inch (20-cm) square sheets of decorative paper

4 photos cut into 4-inch (10-cm) diamonds

paper hole punch

4 12-inch (30-cm) long wooden dowels, ¼-inch (.6-cm) diameter

craft glue

1 2x12-inch (5x30-cm) strip of scrapbook paper

¼x12-inch (.6x30-cm) strips of decorative paper

needle and thread

Create the star bursts:

1. Accordion fold a strip of decorative paper into 12 or more equal segments.

2. Poke a needle and thread through all the folds on one side. Pull the string tight to gather the folds into a wheel with the threaded folds in the center of the circle. Tie the string in a knot and cut the ends short. Secure the knot with a drop of glue.

3. Use a pencil to open the outer folds. Glue the star to the front of the frame.

4. Repeat steps 1–3 to create as many star bursts as you want.

Time Capsule

Freeze a moment in time with this paper craft project. Fill the time capsule with mementos from this year, then stash it away to rediscover years from now.

1. Cut a piece of metallic paper the length and circumference of the tube. If your tube has a cap that comes down over the top, cut a piece to cover the cap too.

2. Glue the paper around the tube and cap.

3. Cut words and dates from an old calendar. Glue them around the tube to form borders.

4. Use alphabet stickers to spell the words "Time Capsule" and the year on the center of the tube.

5. Use other stickers or shape cut-outs to decorate the tube, if desired.

Materials:

metallic papers

cylindrical mailer or poster tube

craft glue

old calendar pages

alphabet stickers

other stickers or small paper cut-outs (optional)

2-inch (5-cm) circle paper punch or a can for tracing

paper hole punch

thin ribbon

6. Use your paper punch to cut out two circles from metallic paper. (You can also cut your circles by hand, using a can for tracing.)

7. Use stickers or a marker to put "Do not open until" on one circle. Put a year for opening your time capsule on the other circle.

8. Punch a hole on the edge of each circle. Tie the circles together with ribbon.

9. Glue the ribbon around the top of the time capsule, letting the circles dangle.

10. Put mementos from the year, predictions, and written memories inside your time capsule. Put it someplace safe until it's time to open it!

Initially Quilled

Special events color your life. Let the programs or flyers from those events color your room. This decoration uses a paper craft skill called quilling. It might take some time to master, but the results will be well worth it.

1. Cut your flyers or programs into ⅛-inch (.3-cm) wide strips. A paper cutter or paper shredder make quick work of this. But you can use a ruler and scissors too.

2. In a word processing program, type the letter you want to quill. Enlarge the letter so it fills the page. Print it out, and cut out the letter. This is your stencil.

3. Trace the stencil onto the center of the card stock.

4. Place a line of glue around the outline of the letter. Hold a paper strip on its edge. Curve and bend it along the lines to create a "wall" around the letter. Hold it in place until it's set. Continue building paper walls around the entire letter. Let dry.

5. Squeeze a small puddle of glue onto scrap paper.

6. Insert a paper strip into the slotted quilling tool. Hold the tool with your dominant hand, and rest the tool on your other hand's forefinger. Roll the tool to quill the paper. When you get to the end, hold the rolled strip securely using your thumb and middle finger. Push the paper roll off the tool.

7. Use the quilling needle to apply glue to the rolled paper end. Press and hold until secure.

8. Grab the quilled shape with tweezers, and dip the bottom edges in glue. Place the shape inside the walls of the letter.

9. Continue filling in the letter with quilled shapes, allowing some tails of paper to curl up off the paper for a 3-D effect. Let the project dry completely.

10. Place the mat board over the project, and then frame for a finished look.

Flowering Friends

Give your space flair with these scented photo flowers. You'll have plenty of room for all your buds.

1. On card stock, draw and cut out a flower petal that measures 2 inches (5 cm) long, 2 inches (5 cm) at the widest part, and ¾ inch (2 cm) wide at the bottom. This is your template.

2. Use your template to trace seven petals onto the back of one sheet of decorative paper. Then cut out the petals.

3. Fold one petal in half the long way, pattern side out. Accordion fold each edge to the center fold. Repeat on the rest of the petals.

4. From a different piece of decorative paper, punch a 1-inch (2.5-cm) circle and a 2-inch (5-cm) circle.

5. Punch a 1½-inch (4-cm) circle from a photo.

6. Squeeze hot glue onto the center of the 1-inch (2.5-cm) circle. Arrange the petals evenly around the circle, with the small ends in the hot glue. Flatten the petals slightly.

7. Squeeze hot glue on the back side of the 2-inch (5-cm) circle. Press it on top of the flower where the petals come together. Then glue the photo circle to this circle.

8. Repeat steps 2–7 to create as many flowers as you'd like.

9. Hot glue the flowers onto branches. Arrange the branches in a pail or vase filled with sand or pebbles.

10. Spritz the backs of your flowers with a summerlike scent that reminds you of your friends.

Materials:

scrap piece of card stock

decorative paper in several different colors or patterns

1-inch (2.5-cm), 1½-inch (4-cm), and 2-inch (5-cm) circle paper punches (or small round objects for tracing)

photos of friends

hot glue

dry tree branches

large pail or vase

sand or pebbles

perfume

Expanding Idea Book

Have an idea you don't want to forget? Need a place to jot down things to do? Use this handy book for all your notes, and you'll always have a record of how far you've come.

1. Glue one of the decorative papers to one cardboard piece. The paper should overhang the cardboard by ½ inch (1 cm) on every side. Fold the overhanging paper over the edges and glue to the back of the cardboard.

2. Glue an index card to the back of the cardboard over the paper edges.

3. Repeat steps 1–2 with the second piece of cardboard and paper.

4. Stick the adhesive cork to the front of one cardboard piece. Use decorative-edge scissors to cut a square from scrap paper. Write a title on the paper, and glue the paper to the cork. Decorate the cork with pins, tacks and other office supplies.

5. Punch holes in the front and back covers ½ inch (1 cm) from the top edge and 1 inch (2.5 cm) from the left and right edges. Punch holes in the same locations on your index cards, using the front cover as a guide.

6. Lay a piece of packing tape across the bottom edge of one index card, extending the tape 1 inch (2.5 cm) out from the right edge. Fold the tape back on itself to make a tab.

7. Use decorative-edge scissors to cut a small label from scrap paper. Write a category title on it. Glue the label to the packing tape tab.

8. Repeat steps 6–7 to make other category pages. Shift the place where you put the tape so that each tab sticks out in a different place on the right edge of the card.

9. Load the back cover, index cards, category pages, and front cover onto the two book rings. Close the rings.

10. Start filling those index cards with reminders, notes, recipes, and lists!

Materials:

craft glue

2 5x7-inch (13x18-cm) pieces of decorative paper

2 4x6-inch (10x15-cm) pieces of cardboard

20–30 4x6-inch (10x15-cm) index cards

3x5-inch (8x13-cm) sheet of adhesive cork

decorative-edge scissors

scrap paper

permanent marker

pins, tacks, or other decorations for the cover

paper hole punch

printed packing tape

2 1-inch (2.5-cm) metal book rings

Tips: If you fill up all the index cards, just open the rings and add more!

Read More

Green, Gail D. *Pretty Presents: Paper Creations to Share*. Paper Creations. North Mankato, Minn.: Capstone Press, 2013.

Lynton, Jeanette R. *Originals: Handcrafted Cards Made Easy*. Salt Lake City: Gibbs Smith, 2008.

Ricketson, Kathreen, ed. *Papercraft: 25 Projects for a Crafty Afternoon*. Kids' Crafternoon. London: Hardie Grant Books, 2011.

Internet Sites

FactHound offers a safe, fun way to find Internet sites related to this book. All of the sites on FactHound have been researched by our staff.

Here's all you do:

Visit *www.facthound.com*

Type in this code: 9781620650448

Super-cool stuff! Check out projects, games and lots more at **www.capstonekids.com**

Author Bio

Kara Laughlin spent much of her childhood making journals, so it only makes sense that she'd grow up to write about art, crafts, and the people who make them. Through her business, Crewelwhorled, she has sold her hand-embroidered jewelry, art, and gifts for nearly 10 years. She has written for *The Crafts Report*, *CraftsBusiness*, and *FiberArts* magazines, and her books, *Beautiful Bags for the Crafty Fashionista* and *Hip Hair Accessories for the Crafty Fashionista* were published by Capstone in 2012.

Snap Books are published by Capstone Press, 1710 Roe Crest Drive, North Mankato, Minnesota 56003. www.capstonepub.com

Library of Congress Cataloging-in-Publication Data
Laughlin, Kara L.
Marvelous memories : paper keepsake creations / by Kara L. Laughlin.
 p. cm.—(Snap books. Paper creations.)
 Includes bibliographical references and index.
 Summary: "Step-by-step instructions teach readers how to create keepsakes with paper"—Provided by publisher.
 ISBN 978-1-62065-044-8 (library binding)
 ISBN 978-1-4765-1788-9 (eBook PDF)
 1. Paper work—Juvenile literature. I. Title.
 TT870.L327 2013
 745.54—dc23   2012020251

Editor: **Jennifer Besel**
Designer: **Tracy Davies McCabe**
Project and Photo Stylist: **Brent Bentrott**
Project Production: **Taylor Olson**
Prop Preparation: **Sarah Schuette**
Scheduler: **Marcy Morin**

Photo Credits:
All photos by Capstone Studio/Karon Dubke, except Shutterstock: YanLev, 18 (inset photo)

Artistic Effects:
Shutterstock: fanny71, HAKKI ARSLAN, Itana, jojof, Labetskiy Alexandr Alexandrovich, Lichtmeister, Magenta10, mama-art, Marina Koven, Nils Z, Polina Katritch, vector-RGB

Printed in the United States of America in North Mankato, Minnesota.
092012   006933CGS13